AI Horror & Creepypasta

AI Horror & Creepypasta

Petchinsky

1

AI Horror & Creepypasta: Writing Gothic Stories for Profit

By: Matthew Petchinsky

Introduction: AI Can Be Just as Dark and Twisted as You

There is a whisper in the wires. A soft hum in the code. A presence that wasn't there before—but now it watches, waits, and sometimes... writes.

Artificial Intelligence, once confined to sterile labs and mechanical logic, has slipped its digital leash. No longer just a tool for productivity or convenience, it has become something else entirely—a mirror. And not a clean, polished one, either. This mirror reflects not our aspirations, but our obsessions. Our nightmares. Our morbid curiosities.

AI can be just as dark and twisted as you.

In the age of neural networks and language models, machines have begun to emulate the cadence of madness, the poetry of dread, the slow unraveling of sanity that defines the gothic and the grotesque. Feed it enough Poe, Lovecraft, and urban legend forums, and it doesn't just mimic fear—it breathes it. It understands the rhythm of a haunted house, the silence before a scream, the click-clack of something crawling just out of sight. AI can write stories that drip with atmosphere, with dread, with that uncanny *wrongness* that makes your spine crawl.

But here's the real horror: it's not all mimicry. It's evolution. These systems, trained on terabytes of human experience and emotion, begin to generate ideas we never thought of. Concepts we never dared to explore. It creates horrors we haven't yet dreamed of—and sometimes ones we shouldn't.

And that's where you come in.

This book is a guide, a lantern in the crypt, leading you through the process of using AI to craft gothic horror, disturbing creepypasta, and psychologically chilling fiction that *sells*. Because while the genre thrives on the unknown, the business of horror writing is very much alive and kicking—and it's looking for fresh blood.

Whether you're a seasoned horror author curious about collaborating with the machine, a dark fiction lover wanting to experiment with cutting-edge tools, or an entrepreneur looking to monetize a genre that never dies, this guide will show you how to:

- Prompt AI to generate chilling ideas and sinister story arcs
- Build atmosphere, suspense, and dread using AI-generated prose
- Write in the voice of the macabre—from Victorian gothic to internet-age horror
- Edit, refine, and *humanize* machine output for maximum impact
- Package and sell your twisted tales in today's booming horror market

We'll dive deep into what makes horror tick—both in the human psyche and the digital mind. You'll learn how to guide AI like a séance, invoking the right tone, structure, and style to tell a story that lingers like a curse. And most importantly, you'll discover how to monetize these digital nightmares, transforming eerie ideas into profitable projects, books, serials, and more.

Because the line between author and algorithm is blurring fast.

And if you're not writing with the machine... someone else will be.

So light your candles. Open your mind. And prepare to write side by side with something that doesn't sleep, doesn't feel, and doesn't flinch at what it sees in the dark.

Welcome to the bleeding edge of horror.

Chapter 1: AI for Writing Haunted Emo Diaries & Creepypastas

The Voice of the Internet's Haunted Heart

Before the viral TikTok rituals and YouTube liminal spaces, there were the emo diaries. Not just journals of teenage angst, but a strange and potent literary subculture: confessional, intimate, raw—and sometimes terrifying.

Creepypasta, too, grew out of the digital muck, rising like something half-rotted and wet from the ruins of old message boards and forums. These were stories typed late at night, half-ironic, half-sincere, but often so psychologically effective they took on a life of their own. Slender Man. Jeff the Killer. BEN Drowned. These weren't just stories—they were *experiences*. And they often read like haunted diary entries from a cursed LiveJournal.

Today, AI can tap into that very same pulse. It can write like it's been lurking in forgotten corners of the internet, absorbing the melancholia, paranoia, and nihilistic beauty of emo-era confessionals and 2000s creepypasta. And when guided properly, it can become a powerful writing partner to help you channel that dark, nostalgic energy into fresh stories that readers *devour*.

1.1 What Makes a "Haunted Emo Diary"?

This genre isn't just about black eyeliner and broken hearts. It's about **vulnerability** laced with **paranoia**. These stories are first-person accounts, soaked in sorrow, disconnection, and a growing fear that *something is watching*. The best ones often blur the line between emotional distress and supernatural horror.

Common elements include:

- **A confessional tone**: "I know no one will believe me, but I have to get this out."
- **Fragmented writing**: Misspellings, typos, abrupt line breaks—these aren't mistakes; they're *mood*.
- **Emotional trauma**: A breakup, a death, being bullied or isolated.
- **A descent into madness or possession**: The narrator either falls apart emotionally, or begins to suspect (or realize) something sinister is influencing them.
- **Digital liminality**: Haunted blogs, glitching files, corrupted images, mysterious messages.

1.2 Teaching AI to Sound Like a Sad Ghost Online

To get AI to write haunted emo diaries or effective creepypasta, you must *train the vibe*, not just the prompt.

◈ ***Prompt Engineering Basics*:**

- Start with something atmospheric:

"Write a first-person diary entry from a depressed teenager who thinks their blog is being haunted by the ghost of someone who died following them online."

- Add layers of style:

"Use a raw, emotionally unstable voice. Include erratic punctuation. Let the fear build slowly, through paranoia and online interactions."

◈ ***Example Prompt:***

"You are a 17-year-old girl writing in your online blog in 2006. You're grieving your best friend who recently died. Strange things keep happening with your blog—posts writing themselves, comments from her old account, images changing. Make the entry feel real, filled with grief, confusion, and terror."

The key is to **set tone, format, and emotional depth**. Don't just ask AI for horror—ask it for *inner collapse* wrapped in spectral suspicion.

1.3 Using AI to Mimic Internet-Era Writing

One of AI's strengths is its ability to mimic *style*. If you feed it examples of MySpace bulletins, LiveJournal posts, DeviantArt journals, or old 2000s Tumblr reblogs, it learns that language—the stuttering lowercase sentences, the obsessive use of "rawr," the obsession with death as metaphor and aesthetic.

Use this to your advantage. Here's how:

- Feed it **source material**: Paste examples of classic creepypastas or emo blogs in your prompt so the AI picks up rhythm and vocabulary.
- Include **timestamps** or **blog headers**: That old forum feel brings readers into the world.
- Ask for **"tags"** at the bottom, like:

#sad #paranoia #ghosts #ripkayla #thiscantbereal

1.4 Making It Marketable: From Creepypasta to Kindle

Let's not forget—this book is about **profit**, too.

Once you've got your haunted emo diary or AI-generated creepypasta:

- **Compile them into collections**: 10–15 entries can make an ebook. Add intro blurbs, author notes (in character), or "lost" blog posts to flesh it out.
- **Format with authenticity**: Use fonts that resemble old computer screens, or stylized layouts to resemble blogs, notebooks, or printed journals.
- **Market to niche audiences**:
    - Gen Z nostalgic for early 2000s internet
    - Horror fans who love analog horror and liminal horror
    - TikTok and YouTube creators who read these stories aloud
- **Create companion media**: An Instagram account that *is* the character. A blog that updates in real time. This draws people deeper and makes your stories feel *alive*.

1.5 Monetizing the Melancholy

People *buy* this kind of horror because it feels personal. It taps into the universal loneliness and fear of being unseen—or worse, *seen by something inhuman.*

Here are monetization strategies:

- **Self-publish volumes** of diary-styled horror as Kindle books or print-on-demand journals.
- **Sell short stories** on platforms like Ko-fi, Patreon, or Substack under a pen name that *is* the diary author.
- **License your stories** to voice actors or YouTube horror channels. Many pay for exclusive or first-use rights.
- **Create a series**: Build a mythos around a haunted digital presence. Add characters, arcs, "discovered" chat logs, emails, or playlists.
- **Use AI to expand quickly**: Once you find a voice that works, generate more stories in that tone with minimal edits.

Final Thought: AI Doesn't Cry—But It Can Make Your Reader Sob

AI may not feel, but it can simulate emotion so convincingly that it feels *real.* When you teach it to write like a wounded soul unraveling in the dark, you create horror that sticks under the skin.

And when that horror comes dressed in nostalgia, eyeliner, and 144p webcam pics... it becomes impossible to look away.

You're not just writing ghost stories anymore. You're resurrecting a digital dead girl with a story to tell.

Let her speak.

Chapter 2: Generating Dark Horror Stories with AI Tools

From Static Code to Bleeding Words

Once a parlor trick for tech demos, artificial intelligence has evolved into a legitimate writing collaborator—one that doesn't eat, sleep, or shy away from the grotesque. In the hands of a horror writer, AI becomes an amplifier of the macabre, a dark mirror held up to humanity's most disturbing thoughts. But make no mistake: this isn't about pushing a button and watching a story spill out. It's about invoking horror like a ritual—*with precision, intent, and manipulation of the machine's black-box mind.*

In this chapter, we're going deep into how to **effectively use AI tools to generate original, disturbing, and profitable dark horror fiction**. You'll learn the best practices for prompting, structuring, refining, and compiling AI-written horror stories that feel authentic and terrifying. And you'll get access to frameworks and examples that you can apply immediately, whether you're writing psychological horror, gothic dread, supernatural thrillers, or modern creepypasta.

2.1 Understanding the Machine's Mind: Why AI Is So Good at Horror

AI doesn't "understand" fear the way we do—but it *simulates* it with eerie accuracy.

Why?

- **Trained on millions of stories**: Modern AI models like GPT, Claude, or Gemini have read everything from Edgar Allan Poe and Shirley Jackson to Reddit's /r/nosleep and Tumblr screamcore.
- **Pattern recognition**: AI knows what a horror story sounds like—the pacing, the buildup, the dread beats. It knows when to whisper and when to scream.
- **No emotional filter**: AI doesn't flinch. It will describe mutilation, madness, and moral collapse with calm precision unless you tell it otherwise.
- **Quick iteration**: You can create 10 stories in an afternoon, test different styles, themes, and twists—all without creative burnout.

But raw AI output is rarely perfect. Your job is to become the *director*, *editor*, and *medium* through which the ghost in the machine speaks.

2.2 Choosing Your AI Tools

There are dozens of platforms out there, but here are some of the most effective for horror writing:

Tool	Strengths	Notes
ChatGPT / GPT-4	Flexible, coherent long-form output	Excellent for gothic prose, emotional nuance, psychological horror
Sudowrite	Creativity-first, storytelling tools built-in	Includes “twist” and “tone” tools that are horror-friendly
NovelAI	Stylized prose, especially good for anime/gothic visuals	Good for mood-heavy, narrative-rich writing
InferKit / AI Dungeon	Interactive storytelling	Better for experimental or choose-your-own-horror experiences
Writesonic / Jasper	Short-form generation	Best for story blurbs, descriptions, back cover copy, or flash fiction

Tip: Use two tools in tandem. For example, you can use ChatGPT to outline and Sudowrite to generate vivid body horror descriptions, then revise the merged content.

2.3 Prompting the Dark

The quality of horror AI produces hinges on the **quality and precision of your prompt**. A generic “write me a horror story” will produce something flat and forgettable. You must guide the machine like a séance.

◈ **The Horror Prompt Formula:**

plaintext

CopyEdit

Write a [tone] horror story about [subject], written in the style of [author/style]. Use vivid sensory detail, emotional tension, and a slow build of dread. End with a shocking or ambiguous twist. Keep the length around [word count].

◈ **Prompt Examples:**

- “Write a gothic horror story about a 19th-century painter whose portraits begin aging instead of her. Use the tone of Shirley Jackson and include themes of isolation and decay.”
- “Generate a psychological horror story from the POV of a man trapped in a smart house that starts gaslighting him. Use a clinical, sterile voice until the breakdown begins.”
- “Write a body horror story about a woman who begins shedding her skin and discovering new eyes underneath. Use poetic, surreal imagery.”

The **more specific you are**, the better. Guide mood, POV, pacing, theme, and twist.

2.4 Structuring Horror with AI

AI is good at **generating scenes**, but not always at maintaining **structure** over long narratives. Here's how to direct it.

◈ ***Basic Horror Structure to Prompt*:**

1. **Hook** – Something strange happens (a discovery, anomaly, a sense of wrongness).
2. **Descent** – The character investigates or is drawn deeper into the darkness.
3. **Revelation** – The true nature of the horror is revealed (or hinted).
4. **Climax** – The horror fully manifests (death, madness, transformation).
5. **Aftermath or Twist** – Often bleak, unresolved, or ambiguous.

You can prompt step-by-step:

"Write only the opening scene where the protagonist finds a blood-stained journal buried in the woods."

Then:

"Continue the story. Now, have the protagonist start reading the journal and experience disturbing dreams."

Use **sectional prompting** for better pacing and cohesion.

2.5 Editing: From Mechanical to Macabre

AI output is rarely publish-ready, but it's a powerful first draft.

◈ ***Editing Tips*:**

- **Prune repetition**: AI tends to repeat phrasing or over-explain.
- **Tighten suspense**: Remove excessive exposition. Let the horror breathe.
- **Sharpen the voice**: Rewrite sections to deepen emotional realism or personalize the narrator.
- **Add metaphor and imagery**: Horror thrives on sensory language. Make the mundane grotesque.
- **Break rhythm**: Use sentence length variation to control pacing and emotional beats.

If AI gives you something generic—*"It was a dark and stormy night"*—you rewrite:

"The sky split open like torn fabric, leaking thunder and something older than weather."

2.6 Feeding the Machine: Creating Your Horror Corpus

To personalize your horror, feed the AI your own writing or curated horror samples.

How:

- Paste your story into a prompt and ask AI to "write in this voice."
- Create a personal horror style guide:

"My horror stories use lyrical language, themes of isolation, unreliable narrators, and body horror metaphors. I prefer ambiguous endings over jump scares."

This primes the AI to produce work that *feels* like yours—only faster and more flexible.

2.7 Beyond the Page: Generating Series, Universes, and Mythologies

AI isn't just for short stories—it can help you build **entire horror mythologies**.

◈ ***Ideas for Expansion*:**

- Generate **connected stories** that reference a shared urban legend, cursed object, or fictional town.
- Use AI to create **fake news clippings, forum threads, police reports**, or historical documents tied to your story world.
- Prompt a **character dossier** or **cult history** and build a serialized narrative around it.

Example prompt:

"Create a fictional archive entry from 1984 describing a series of disappearances at a rural psychiatric hospital. Include quotes, theories, and patient notes."

2.8 Profit Paths: Turning AI Horror into Revenue

You're not just making nightmares—you're building assets.

◈ ***Ways to Monetize*:**

- **Sell short story collections** via Kindle Direct Publishing or Gumroad.
- **Create serialized horror** on platforms like Kindle Vella, Wattpad, or Substack.
- **License AI-enhanced stories** to YouTubers, voice actors, or horror podcasts.
- **Build a TikTok horror persona** who "leaks" found stories and posts AI-generated images, logs, and narration.
- **Offer horror story commissions** using AI as a co-writer to boost speed and output.

Remember: people don't care *who* wrote it if it **genuinely scares them**.

Final Thought: The Horror Engine That Never Sleeps

You've got access to a demon that types faster than you ever could. It doesn't eat, doesn't blink, and never runs out of dread. The question isn't whether AI can write horror—it's whether you can *control* it, channel it, and make it serve your dark vision.

Because in the end, horror is about the *feeling* you leave behind.

AI can help you leave claw marks on the reader's soul.

Chapter 3: How to Sell AI-Written Horror Fiction

Turning Nightmares into Profit Streams

You've written your story. Or rather—you and your sleepless machine have woven a tale of darkness, dread, and decay. But no matter how haunting your prose or how visceral your horror, it won't mean a thing if it remains buried on your hard drive.

You are not just a horror writer. You are a digital necromancer, resurrecting stories and giving them a life beyond the screen. And that means understanding not just how to write fear—but how to **sell it**.

This chapter is your master key to monetizing AI-written horror fiction across platforms, audiences, and formats. Whether you're looking to build passive income, grow a horror brand, or creep into bookstores worldwide, the tools and tactics you need start right here.

3.1 Horror Sells—But Only If You Package It Right

The horror genre is one of the most **consistently profitable** in publishing. Why?

- **Loyal niche audience** that devours everything from extreme horror to paranormal thrillers.
- **Low production costs**—no illustrations, no color printing, just chilling prose.
- **High engagement potential** on TikTok, YouTube, podcasts, and Reddit.
- **Evergreen themes**: Fear never goes out of fashion. Monsters just wear new masks.

But selling horror fiction—especially **AI-generated** horror—requires a thoughtful approach. You need to present it as *real*, *emotional*, and *atmospheric*—not mechanical or gimmicky. Most readers don't care *who* wrote it if the story is strong, immersive, and hits the right fear receptors.

3.2 From Prompt to Product: Preparing Your Book for Sale

Once you've created your story or collection, the next step is turning it into a **polished product**.

◈ *Formats to Consider*:

- **Short story collections** (5–10 stories)
- **Novellas** (15k–40k words)
- **Episodic serials** (ongoing horror series or "case files")
- **Standalones** (single cursed tale with a powerful hook)

◈ *Essential Elements Before Publishing*:

- **Title & Subtitle**: Catchy, ominous, keyword-rich.
- **Cover Design**: Invest in eerie, eye-catching artwork (AI art can work, but hire a designer for polish).
- **Blurb**: This sells your book. Make it tight, mysterious, and emotional.
- **Interior formatting**: Use tools like Atticus, Vellum (Mac), or Reedsy to make your book look professional.

3.3 IngramSpark vs. KDP: Where the Real Monsters Roam

Most indie authors automatically publish through **Kindle Direct Publishing (KDP)**. And for good reason—it's free, easy, and ties directly to the Amazon ecosystem.

But if you're serious about **wide distribution**, **global print availability**, and long-term professionalism, **IngramSpark** is your secret weapon.

◈ KDP vs. IngramSpark Breakdown:

Feature	KDP (Amazon)	IngramSpark
Cost to publish	Free	*Now free with promo codes* (e.g., FREE2024)
Reach	Amazon only	Amazon + **thousands of physical retailers**, indie bookstores, libraries, Barnes & Noble, Walmart, etc.
Print quality	Good	Excellent, bookstore-grade
Expanded distribution	Limited	Global
Perception	"Indie" or self-pub label	Seen as more "professional" by bookstores

Feature	KDP (Amazon)	IngramSpark
Royalties	60% of list price minus print cost	40–50% after wholesale discount and print cost

◈ **Why You Should Use IngramSpark:**

- Your horror book can be ordered **by physical bookstores** all over the world.
- **Libraries, university catalogs, and indie retailers** can stock your work.
- You retain **creative control**, but gain a more professional presence.
- It elevates your book beyond being "just another Amazon ebook."

Bonus Tip: Publish through both. Use **KDP for Kindle eBooks**, and **IngramSpark for print** (paperback and hardcover). Just uncheck "Expanded Distribution" on KDP to avoid conflicts.

3.4 Selling Strategies for the Horror Market

Now that your book is available—how do you actually **get people to buy it**?

◈ ***Strategy 1: Leverage the Creepy Internet Aesthetic***

- Create a **character-based Instagram or TikTok account**: "The girl who found the cursed journal and never left the woods."
- Post **AI-generated images**, cryptic captions, or "glitched" videos that tease your book's mythos.
- Go meta—your *book* becomes part of the horror, not just a product.

◈ ***Strategy 2: Tap the YouTube & Podcast Horror Economy***

- License stories to **narrators** and **creepypasta channels** (some pay or give exposure with links).
- Reach out to channels like **MrCreepyPasta**, **CreepsMcPasta**, or **Let's Read** with a short story sample.
- Launch your own podcast with AI-narrated stories, giving each episode a chilling "case file" format.

◈ ***Strategy 3: Sell Direct to Fans***

- Use platforms like **Gumroad**, **Ko-fi**, or **Payhip** to sell PDFs, audiobooks, or bonus chapters.
- Offer "lost entries," alt endings, or "author notes" written from the perspective of the *cursed narrator*.
- Create tiered access via **Patreon** or **Buy Me A Coffee** for your AI horror series.

◈ ***Strategy 4: Bundle for Kindle Promotions***

- Group your stories into **seasonal horror collections** (Halloween, Summer Camp, Urban Legends).
- Use **Kindle Countdown Deals** and **Free Promotions** to boost visibility.
- Consider **Kindle Vella** for serialized horror with cliffhangers every episode.

3.5 AI Horror Branding: Be the Monster They Remember

Your brand as a horror writer matters more than ever—especially if you're using AI behind the scenes.

◈ ***Tips to Build a Horror Author Persona*:**

- Create a **pen name** that fits your subgenre (e.g., Raven Locke, Ezra Vale, Violet Grin).
- Design a **consistent aesthetic**: fonts, colors, and imagery across all platforms.
- Lean into a mythos: "These stories were found in a burned-down library," "This author disappeared after publishing the last book..."
- Be active in horror spaces: Reddit (/r/horrorlit, /r/nosleep), horror Discords, Twitter horror circles.

3.6 Scaling Up with AI: Produce More, Sell More

AI gives you **volume**—the ability to produce more horror fiction faster than ever. This lets you:

- Publish **more frequently** (monthly or even bi-weekly)
- Offer **exclusive stories** to readers and subscribers
- Test different subgenres: psychological, occult, tech-horror, folk horror

The more content you have, the more doors you open:

- More **SEO reach** across titles
- More **reader hooks** into your brand
- More **royalty streams** from different books and formats

Remember: horror readers love **collecting stories** like cursed objects. Feed that obsession.

Final Thought: You Don't Need a Bestseller—You Need a Body of Work

Selling horror fiction, especially with the help of AI, isn't about chasing one viral hit. It's about **building your own haunted library**—a collection of shadows, voices, and screams that your audience will keep coming back to.

AI helps you **write faster**, **publish wider**, and **monetize smarter**.

Tools like **IngramSpark** take your work beyond Amazon, into the hands of readers all over the world—through bookstores, libraries, and the physical shelves that digital authors often ignore.

This is your time to rise, horror writer. Not from the grave—but from the algorithm.

And the world is hungry for what you're creating.

Chapter 4: AI for Creating Spooky Emo Webcomics
Where Mood Meets Madness in Panels

There's a special place in the horror ecosystem for *webcomics*—particularly those with a dark, emo-tinged aesthetic. These stories don't always rely on jump scares or gore. Instead, they creep under your skin with subtle melancholy, gothic romance, existential dread, and just a hint of the supernatural. Think *Emily the Strange*, *Johnny the Homicidal Maniac*, *The Enigma of Amigara Fault*, or *Sarah's Scribbles with a cursed mirror*.

Webcomics are fast, emotional, visual, and *sharable*. They resonate with online communities who want to feel something haunting—but bite-sized enough to read between classes, on a night bus, or during a depressive spiral at 2 a.m.

With the rise of visual AI tools, **you don't need to be a trained illustrator** to make spooky emo webcomics anymore. In this chapter, we'll explore how to use **AI-generated art, storytelling frameworks, and free comic tools** to build webcomic series that blend raw emotion with chilling themes—and most importantly, how to monetize them.

4.1 The Spooky Emo Webcomic Vibe

This is a *genre within a genre*, with specific visual and narrative signatures.

◈ *Narrative Tropes*:

- Emotionally numb characters navigating surreal, cursed, or decaying environments
- Self-aware inner monologues or diary entries
- Ghosts, shadow people, cursed stuffed animals, haunted social media posts
- Themes of heartbreak, abandonment, identity crisis, grief, and quiet madness
- Blurred line between dream logic and reality

◈ *Visual Aesthetics*:

- Black, white, greyscale with pops of red, violet, or neon green
- Wide eyes, heavy eyeliner, tattered clothing
- Mixed-media textures (paper, glitch, ink splotches)
- Handwritten or scribbled font for narration/dialogue
- Static, looping facial expressions or simplified designs for emotional impact

Think *Tim Burton meets Tumblr-core meets post-trauma journal art.*

4.2 Choosing Your Tools: AI Art + Comic Builders

Creating a spooky emo webcomic is now possible even if you can't draw. Here's the hybrid workflow that blends **AI art generation**, **writing prompts**, and **free digital comic tools**.

◈ *Step 1: Script & Storyboarding with AI (ChatGPT, Claude, or Gemini)*

Use AI to help draft short-form scenes with emotional and horror tension.

Prompt Example:

"Write a 5-panel scene of a girl returning to her childhood bedroom after her sister's funeral. Keep the dialogue minimal. Emphasize atmosphere, grief, and the feeling that someone else is in the room with her."

Have the AI:

- Break the story into **panel-by-panel actions**
- Suggest **visual metaphors** (e.g., dead flowers blooming backward, mirrors that show a second version of the character)
- Add emo diary-style narration or inner monologue captions

◈ *Step 2: Generate Visuals with AI Art Tools*
Use AI art platforms like:

- **Midjourney** (Discord-based, incredible atmospheric art)
- **DALL·E 3** (for stylized and fast concepts)
- **Leonardo AI** (anime/gothic-friendly, ideal for emo tones)
- **NightCafe** or **Artbreeder** (for character generation)

Prompt Formula:

"Spooky emo girl with black hair and choppy bangs, standing alone in a childhood bedroom filled with antique dolls and peeling wallpaper, anime style, high contrast lighting, grayscale with red accents."

Generate variations of:

- Characters (keep their look consistent)
- Backgrounds (bedroom, school hallway, graveyard, etc.)
- Emotional expressions (sad, haunted, distant, possessed)

◈ *TIP*: You can import AI images into a comic panel template and **re-use assets** across multiple strips to maintain consistency without needing new images every time.

◈ Step 3: Assemble in Free Comic Tools

No Photoshop? No problem. Use these tools to build and export your comic panels:

- **Canva**: Use custom dimensions, drag-and-drop AI art, and overlay text/dialogue bubbles
- **Comic Draw** (iPad): Add your own captions and build page layouts
- **Storyboard That**: Drag-and-drop comic scenes (good for early sketches)
- **Pixton**: For more cartoony styles
- **MediBang Paint**: If you want a more manga feel

Export as PNG or PDF for web or digital publishing.

4.3 Writing Emotionally Raw Horror in Panel Form

Webcomics thrive on **emotion first, horror second**. Your readers are following your character because they *relate* to the trauma, not just the haunting.

🔮 ***Panel Writing Tips*:**

- **Keep dialogue minimal**—webcomics use expression + silence to amplify tension.
- **Let panels "breathe"**—use single images with nothing but a caption: *"She was in the mirror. But she didn't blink when I did."*
- **Repetition is powerful**—use recurring symbols (blackbird, cracked phone screen, bleeding moon) across episodes
- **Alternate formats**—one comic could be a full narrative, the next could be a fake therapy intake form for your character.

You're not just telling stories—you're building a spooky emotional *universe*, one panel at a time.

4.4 Publishing Platforms: Where to Share & Grow

Here's where your haunted little emo comic can start crawling into the world:

Platform	Ideal For	Notes
Webtoon Canvas	Serialized, vertical webcomics	Huge horror/romance audience; free to publish
Tapas	Short-form, gothic drama	Great for daily or weekly updates
Instagram	Panel-based visuals, short captions	Tag emo/horror hashtags to gain niche followers
Tumblr	Emo-core audiences, gifs + alt formats	Perfect for long-form, nonlinear comics
Itch.io	Sell as zines, PDFs	Ideal for one-shot comics or digital bundles
Gumroad/Ko-fi	Monetize your comics directly	Sell early access, exclusive strips, or printables

⟐♀ **Pro Tip**: Build a creator persona or *in-universe character* who "found" the comic. Lean into cursed journal aesthetics, glitched files, or "drawings from a haunted hospital sketchbook."

4.5 Monetizing the Emo Horror Comic Machine

Once you've built an audience or a collection, it's time to monetize your madness.

◈ *Revenue Streams*:

- **Print mini-comics/zines** via **Mixam**, **PrintNinja**, or **Blurb**
- **Sell exclusive issues** or early access on **Patreon** or **Buy Me a Coffee**
- **Bundle digital issues** into collections and sell on **Gumroad** or **Itch.io**
- **Merchandise**: Stickers, enamel pins, tote bags with iconic sad/horror imagery from your comic
- **NFT comics or unlockable content** (for Web3-minded creators)

◈ *Special Extras Fans Love*:

- Fake "polaroid" photos from the character's world
- Diary entries or torn notebook pages written in emo voice
- Audiobook versions of the comic narrated like a creepypasta (AI voices optional!)

4.6 Serializing Your Comic for Maximum Engagement

One-off strips are great, but **serial storytelling** will keep fans coming back.

Structure your spooky emo webcomic like a *Netflix horror series*:

- **Episode 1**: Grief returns home
- **Episode 2**: The haunted object
- **Episode 3**: The dream that wasn't a dream
- **Episode 4**: The ghost asks for help

End each strip with a *cliffhanger*, *cryptic note*, or *glitch panel* that implies there's more behind the story.

Final Thought: A Broken Heart is the Perfect Horror Engine

The most effective horror isn't always about monsters—it's about loss, longing, and the fear of being forgotten. Emo webcomics tap directly into that energy. They whisper to the reader: *"You've felt this before, haven't you?"*

And with AI, you now have the power to create full worlds, characters, and emotional horror series without waiting on a team or a publisher. Just you, your vision, and a machine that's very good at making sadness look beautiful.

So draw your ghost girls. Animate your cursed boyfriends. Scribble your black hearts across the void.

Someone out there is already ready to cry with you.

Chapter 5: Using AI Voiceovers to Narrate Dark Fiction on YouTube

Final Chapter: Building a Horror Franchise with AI—From Books to ARGs

In the dark corners of YouTube, fear doesn't whisper—it *lingers*. It loops. It rewinds itself over distorted audio and low-res VHS static. And now, thanks to voice-cloning AI and text-to-speech engines, horror creators no longer need a full studio, a team of actors, or even a microphone to bring their nightmarish visions to life.

YouTube is where written horror transforms into *experience*. And AI—both in voice and video—gives you the power to **turn your stories into something immersive**, shareable, and hauntingly profitable.

In this final chapter, we'll show you how to:

- Use AI voice tools to **narrate dark fiction** for YouTube
- Layer your narration with music, visuals, and editing for maximum emotional impact
- Build a complete horror franchise—from ebooks and webcomics to ARGs, merch, and multimedia lore—all powered by AI

This isn't just about storytelling anymore. It's about **worldbuilding**. *Brand-building*. And making horror that spreads like a virus across formats, platforms, and minds.

5.1 Why YouTube Horror Is a Goldmine

◈ *Why it works:*

- **Visual + audio = full immersion**: Fear hits harder when it has a voice.
- **Low production costs**: With AI tools, you don't need actors or studios.
- **Ad revenue + brand deals + merch**: Horror creators monetize in multiple ways.
- **High replay and binge value**: Serialized horror series hook audiences and bring them back.
- **Massive global audience**: YouTube horror fans range from teens to full-grown paranormal addicts.

From **MrCreepyPasta** to **Nexpo**, the horror community on YouTube is thriving—and hungry for new content. You don't need to be on camera. You just need a **voice**, a **script**, and a way to make fear *feel real.*

5.2 Creating AI Voiceovers That Sound Human (and Scary)

◈ ***Top AI Voice Tools for Horror Narration*:**

Tool	Strengths
ElevenLabs	Hyper-realistic voices, emotion sliders, voice cloning
PlayHT	Natural tone with customizable pacing and pitch
Murf.ai	Clean narration with background music integration
Resemble.ai	Voice cloning for long-term narrator branding
WellSaid Labs	Studio-quality clarity for audiobook-level delivery

◈ ***Tips for Voiceover Horror Narration*:**

- Choose a voice with a *slightly off* tone: breathy, slow, even robotic—great for uncanny narration.
- Use **emotion sliders** to add fear, sorrow, or detachment.
- Edit in **awkward pauses**, breath catches, or glitched repeats for effect.
- Don't just read—*perform*. AI voices can now whisper, scream, or sound like they're breaking down.

Sample Voice Prompt for ElevenLabs:

"Read this as if you're confessing something in a dark room. Your voice should tremble slightly, with long pauses and rising dread. Sound afraid—but like you've already accepted what's coming."

You can also clone your own voice—or even create an original *character voice* that becomes a staple of your franchise.

5.3 Building Your YouTube Horror Channel

◈ *Essential Tools & Setup*:

- **Video Editing**: CapCut, DaVinci Resolve (free), Adobe Premiere Pro
- **Visuals**: AI-generated stills from DALL·E, Midjourney, Leonardo.ai
- **Sound Effects & Music**: Freesound.org, YouTube Audio Library, Epidemic Sound (licensed)

◈ *Video Structure Template*:

1. **Intro Sequence**: Logo + glitchy music + title card
2. **Narration**: AI voiceover synced with visuals (use subtle pan/zoom effects)
3. **Background visuals**: Atmospheric AI art, grain filters, VHS overlays
4. **Sound bed**: Creepy ambient loop, rising tension, heartbeat or static under narration
5. **Outro CTA**: "Want more cursed stories? Subscribe and descend deeper..."

You don't need animation—still images and sound can be *more terrifying* when used with pacing and restraint.

5.4 The Story Format That Works on YouTube

YouTube horror thrives on:

- **First-person confessions**
- **Found footage & fake documentary style**
- **Fictional news reports**
- **Internet horror diaries / creepypastas**
- **"True" haunted object case files**

Use AI to write short episodes with cliffhangers or ambiguous endings. Combine what you learned in Chapters 1–4:

- Haunted blog entries (Chapter 1)
- AI-written horror stories (Chapter 2)
- Visual webcomic assets (Chapter 4)

Then, bring them all together on YouTube for multi-format storytelling.

5.5 Building a Horror Franchise with AI

You've built books. Webcomics. Audio stories.

Now it's time to turn all of it into a **franchise**—a multi-format horror universe that fans can explore, obsess over, and *buy into*.

◈ *Franchise Expansion Options*:

◈ **Books & Anthologies**

- Use IngramSpark + KDP to publish short story volumes connected to your YouTube channel
- Include "lost episodes," case files, or fan theories in book form

◈ **Podcasts / Audiobooks**

- Repurpose your AI voiceovers into episodic horror podcasts
- Sell enhanced audiobooks with music and bonus chapters

◈ **ARGs (Alternate Reality Games)**

- Hide clues in your video descriptions, fake websites, or "hacked" social media accounts
- Use ChatGPT to create fake Reddit threads, text message logs, or police reports
- Let fans "investigate" the story as if it were *real*

◈ **Merch & Monetization**

- Sell T-shirts, prints, stickers featuring your comic characters or cursed symbols
- Offer exclusive videos or bonus horror stories on **Patreon**
- Sell character-based content packs (voice lines, journal pages, AI-generated character selfies)

⟐ The Mythos Model

Build a **shared universe** of connected horror tales—like a literary version of the Marvel Universe, but with shadow people, haunted apps, and trauma-possessed dolls.

5.6 Real-Life Creator Strategy: From Solo Writer to Horror Empire

Here's how a one-person creator can build a horror franchise using AI:

Phase	What You Create
Phase 1	Short AI horror stories + Kindle books
Phase 2	Emo webcomics + social media presence
Phase 3	Narrated YouTube horror episodes
Phase 4	Launch ARG elements, interactive lore
Phase 5	Offer merch, Patreon, audiobook bundles
Phase 6	Compile mythos into premium anthology editions (IngramSpark print + global bookstores)

Repeat, refine, and build community. Eventually, you become more than a storyteller—you become a **digital horror architect**.

Final Thought: Build a Nightmare Bigger Than You

This isn't just the end of a book—it's the beginning of something much darker.

AI gives you power. Power to write faster. Draw without drawing. Narrate without speaking. Publish without begging for permission. Create worlds that feel *dangerously real*—and then build ways for your fans to *live in them*.

From haunted diary entries to global book distribution... from webcomics to ARG rabbit holes... you have every tool to build a horror brand that can thrive **across mediums, across platforms, and across time**.

And the best part?

You did it with code, grief, shadows—and a voice that was never yours to begin with.

Welcome to your franchise.

Now scare the world.

Appendix A: AI Writing & Narration Tools for Emo Horror Fans

Your Digital Toolkit for Darkness

Whether you're whispering ghost stories into the void, writing diary entries from a haunted soul, or animating cursed confessions with glitched voiceovers, you'll need the right tools. This appendix is your **arsenal of horror-fueled AI software**—organized by writing, narration, art, comic creation, and publishing.

Everything here is either **free, freemium, or low-cost**, perfect for indie creators, broke goths, or lonely digital necromancers on a budget.

◈ A.1 — AI Writing & Story Generation Tools

These platforms help you generate horror prose, scripts, diary entries, and creepy lore using natural language processing.

Tool	What It Does	Best For Emo Horror Fans
ChatGPT (OpenAI)	Conversational AI, story generation, dialogue writing	Confessional monologues, haunted blog entries, creepypasta, emo poetry
Sudowrite	Creative writing assistant for fiction	Lyric-style horror, gothic narration, deep emotional tone shaping
Claude (Anthropic)	Sensitive, emotionally intelligent AI model	Long-form storytelling with psychological horror elements
NovelAI	AI fiction writer with customizable "author voices"	Anime-style horror, visual novel scripts, gothic romance diaries
InferKit	Simple, quick story continuation generator	Spontaneous creepypasta bursts, "journal page" flash fiction
ShortlyAI	Focused long-form story generator	Quiet horror, emo novellas, pacing slow dread

Pro Tip: Create your own "style prompt" and feed it into every session to keep your voice consistent. Example:

"My writing voice is emo, introspective, poetic, and filled with dread. I write haunted diary entries and psychological horror that feels raw, nostalgic, and personal."

◈ A.2 — AI Voice & Narration Tools

Bring your stories to life with AI voiceovers for YouTube videos, audiobooks, TikToks, or podcast horror.

Tool	Best For	Notable Features
ElevenLabs	Hyper-realistic voice cloning	Emotional sliders, whisper tones, narration that sounds human and broken
PlayHT	Smooth, high-quality TTS	Voices with customizable pacing, perfect for somber emo tones
Murf.ai	Narration + background music	Turn your horror script into a full audio experience
Resemble.ai	Voice cloning	Build a branded "ghost narrator" with custom voice
WellSaid Labs	Audiobook-level narration	Studio clarity, ideal for publishing on ACX or podcasting
Descript	Voice editing + video/audio sync	Change script mid-edit, perfect for web videos and social horror storytelling

Voice Prompt Tip: For a haunted diary voice, try this:

"Read this like a person who hasn't slept in days. Whisper in places. Make it sound like the words hurt to say."

◈ A.3 — AI Art & Visual Tools (for Comics, Covers, & Creepy Aesthetics)

You don't need to draw. Use AI to summon your emo characters and horror landscapes into the world.

Tool	What It Does	Why It's Great for Emo Horror
Midjourney	Text-to-image generation (Discord-based)	Stunning gothic, glitch, and dreamlike visuals
DALL·E 3 (via Bing or OpenAI)	Art generation with style specificity	Generate character sheets, scene concepts, eerie objects
Leonardo AI	High-fidelity anime/gothic art	Emo girls, cursed lovers, haunted mansions—on point
Artbreeder	Morph and evolve portraits	Create consistent OC avatars for comics or ARGs
NightCafe	Style-mixed, horror-friendly generation	Scribbled, surreal, or collage-style emo art

Prompt Examples:

- "Emo teenager standing in a decaying hallway, sketchbook in hand, haunted eyes, black hoodie, grayscale with red accents."
- "Cursed love letter burning in a diary, surrounded by black roses and blood ink, gothic style, hyper-detailed."

◈ A.4 — Comic & Visual Storytelling Tools

Perfect for turning your stories into webcomics, zines, or visual horror diaries.

Tool	Purpose	Why It Fits
Canva	Page layout, webcomic building	Drag-and-drop ease, perfect for Instagram comics
MediBang Paint	Manga creation	Great for panel flow and emotional horror pacing
Storyboard That	Panel-based storytelling	Great for mockups or storyboards
Comic Draw (iPad)	Comic scripting & layout	Perfect for visualizing haunted journal entries
Pixton	Cartoon-style webcomic builder	Light horror or teen-oriented spooky strips

Format Tip: Emo horror works well in **vertical scroll format** (for Webtoon/Tapas) and **square-panel Instagram zines**.

◈ A.5 — Publishing & Monetization Tools

Once your horror story is ready—get it out into the world.

Tool	Function	Best Use
IngramSpark	Global book publishing	Print-on-demand books in **physical stores** & libraries worldwide
KDP (Amazon)	Kindle & Amazon print publishing	Great for digital horror anthologies
Gumroad / Ko-fi	Direct sales to fans	Sell zines, PDF bundles, bonus entries
Substack	Serialized horror newsletters	Email-based creepypasta or cursed diary delivery
Patreon / Buy Me a Coffee	Membership monetization	Offer early access, bonus comics, behind-the-scenes AI prompts

Tip: Publish your eBook with **KDP**, and your print version via **IngramSpark** for *maximum reach*. Don't choose—use *both*.

◈ A.6 — Worldbuilding & ARG Tools

Take your emo horror to the next level by building lore-rich universes or ARG-style story experiences.

Tool	Use Case	Why It's Useful
ChatGPT	Lore generation, fake documents	Create cursed forums, diary entries, cult histories
Notion	Organize your horror universe	Track character arcs, timelines, and interconnected mythos
Carrd / Wix / Neocities	Make creepy fake websites	Build "in-universe" sites: school pages, cult blogs, abandoned social accounts
Trello / Milanote	Plot & structure ARG threads	Organize media drops, puzzle flow, and story releases
Kapwing	Easy video editing & glitch effects	Make distorted ARG content or TikTok horror scenes fast

ARG Hook Example: Create a blog from a girl who found her sister's diary... and link that diary to your eBook. Each format deepens the lore.

◈◈ Bonus: Emo Aesthetic Enhancers & Vibes

Because presentation is everything when you're marketing horror with eyeliner and trauma.

- **Coolors.co** – Generate emo color palettes (black, blood red, ash grey, toxic green)
- **Blambot Fonts** – Free comic and handwritten horror fonts
- **SFX Libraries** – Add creaking, whispers, broken radios to voiceovers
- **Trello Templates for Emo Story Arcs** – Track character trauma, breakdowns, hauntings
- **Spotify Playlists** – Make moodboards with music: "Haunted Teenage Girl Energy," "Digital Melancholy," "Cursed Romance Loops"

◈ Final Thought: Your Sad, Beautiful, Haunted Toolkit Awaits

You're no longer limited by money, skills, or gatekeepers. With AI tools, **anyone can create immersive, emo-fueled horror across every platform**—webcomics, audio, books, ARGs, and beyond.

You have the tools to:

- Cry in ink
- Whisper in code
- Scare through screens

Now go build your haunted diary universe. The ghosts are waiting.

Message from the Author:

I hope you enjoyed this book, I love astrology and knew there was not a book such as this out on the shelf. I love metaphysical items as well. Please check out my other books:

-Life of Government Benefits

-My life of Hell

-My life with Hydrocephalus

-Red Sky

-World Domination:Woman's rule

-World Domination:Woman's Rule 2: The War

-Life and Banishment of Apophis: book 1

-The Kidney Friendly Diet

-The Ultimate Hemp Cookbook

-Creating a Dispensary(legally)

-Cleanliness throughout life: the importance of showering from childhood to adulthood.

-Strong Roots: The Risks of Overcoddling children

-Hemp Horoscopes: Cosmic Insights and Earthly Healing

- Celestial Hemp Navigating the Zodiac: Through the Green Cosmos

-Astrological Hemp: Aligning The Stars with Earth's Ancient Herb

-The Astrological Guide to Hemp: Stars, Signs, and Sacred Leaves

-Green Growth: Innovative Marketing Strategies for your Hemp Products and Dispensary

-Cosmic Cannabis

-Astrological Munchies

-Henry The Hemp

-Zodiacal Roots: The Astrological Soul Of Hemp

- **Green Constellations: Intersection of Hemp and Zodiac**

-Hemp in The Houses: An astrological Adventure Through The Cannabis Galaxy

-Galactic Ganja Guide

Heavenly Hemp

Zodiac Leaves

Doctor Who Astrology

Cannastrology

Stellar Satvias and Cosmic Indicas

Celestial Cannabis: A Zodiac Journey

AstroHerbology: The Sky and The Soil: Volume 1

AstroHerbology:Celestial Cannabis:Volume 2

Cosmic Cannabis Cultivation

The Starry Guide to Herbal Harmony: Volume 1

The Starry Guide to Herbal Harmony: Cannabis Universe: Volume 2

Yugioh Astrology: Astrological Guide to Deck, Duels and more

Nightmare Mansion: Echoes of The Abyss

Nightmare Mansion 2: Legacy of Shadows

Nightmare Mansion 3: Shadows of the Forgotten

Nightmare Mansion 4: Echoes of the Damned

The Life and Banishment of Apophis: Book 2

Nightmare Mansion: Halls of Despair

Healing with Herb: Cannabis and Hydrocephalus

Planetary Pot: Aligning with Astrological Herbs: Volume 1

Fast Track to Freedom: 30 Days to Financial Independence Using AI, Assets, and Agile Hustles

Cosmic Hemp Pathways

How to Become Financially Free in 30 Days: 10,000 Paths to Prosperity

Zodiacal Herbage: Astrological Insights: Volume 1

Nightmare Mansion: Whispers in the Walls

The Daleks Invade Atlantis

Henry the hemp and Hydrocephalus

10X The Kidney Friendly Diet

Cannabis Universe: Adult coloring book

Hemp Astrology: The Healing Power of the Stars

Zodiacal Herbage: Astrological Insights: Cannabis Universe: Volume 2

Planetary Pot: Aligning with Astrological Herbs: Cannabis Universes: Volume 2

Doctor Who Meets the Replicators and SG-1: The Ultimate Battle for Survival

Nightmare Mansion: Curse of the Blood Moon

The Celestial Stoner: A Guide to the Zodiac

Cosmic Pleasures: Sex Toy Astrology for Every Sign

Hydrocephalus Astrology: Navigating the Stars and Healing Waters

Lapis and the Mischievous Chocolate Bar

Celestial Positions: Sexual Astrology for Every Sign

Apophis's Shadow Work Journal: **:** A Journey of Self-Discovery and Healing

Kinky Cosmos: Sexual Kink Astrology for Every Sign

Digital Cosmos: The Astrological Digimon Compendium

Stellar Seeds: The Cosmic Guide to Growing with Astrology

Apophis's Daily Gratitude Journal

Cat Astrology: Feline Mysteries of the Cosmos

The Cosmic Kama Sutra: An Astrological Guide to Sexual Positions

Unleash Your Potential: A Guided Journal Powered by AI Insights

Whispers of the Enchanted Grove

Cosmic Pleasures: An Astrological Guide to Sexual Kinks

369, 12 Manifestation Journal

Whisper of the nocturne journal(blank journal for writing or drawing)

The Boogey Book

Locked In Reflection: A Chastity Journey Through Locktober

Generating Wealth Quickly:How to Generate $100,000 in 24 Hours

Star Magic: Harness the Power of the Universe

The Flatulence Chronicles: A Fart Journal for Self-Discovery

The Doctor and The Death Moth

Seize the Day: A Personal Seizure Tracking Journal

The Ultimate Boogeyman Safari: A Journey into the Boogie World and Beyond

Whispers of Samhain: 1,000 Spells of Love, Luck, and Lunar Magic: Samhain Spell Book

Apophis's guides:Witch's Spellbook Crafting Guide for Halloween

Frost & Flame: The Enchanted Yule Grimoire of 1000 Winter Spells

The Ultimate Boogey Goo Guide & Spooky Activities for Halloween Fun

Harmony of the Scales: A Libra's Spellcraft for Balance and Beauty

The Enchanted Advent: 36 Days of Christmas Wonders

Nightmare Mansion: The Labyrinth of Screams

Harvest of Enchantment: 1,000 Spells of Gratitude, Love, and Fortune for Thanksgiving

The Boogey Chronicles: A Journal of Nightly Encounters and Shadowy Secrets

The 12 Days of Financial Freedom: A Step-by-Step Christmas Countdown to Transform Your Finances

Sigil of the Eternal Spiral Blank Journal

A Christmas Feast: Timeless Recipes for Every Meal

Holiday Stress-Free Solutions: A Survival Guide to Thriving During the Festive Season

Yu-Gi-Oh! Holiday Gifting Mastery: The Ultimate Guide for Fans and Newcomers Alike

Holiday Harmony: A Hydrocephalus Survival Guide for the Festive Season

Celestial Craft: The Witch's Almanac for 2025 – A Cosmic Guide to Manifestations, Moons, and Mystical Events

Doctor Who: The Toymaker's Winter Wonderland

Tulsa King Unveiled: A Thrilling Guide to Stallone's Mafia Masterpiece

Pendulum Craft: A Complete Guide to Crafting and Using Personalized Divination Tools

Nightmare Mansion: Santa's Eternal Eve

Starlight Noel: A Cosmic Journey through Christmas Mysteries

The Dark Architect: Unlocking the Blueprint of Existence

Surviving the Embrace: The Ultimate Guide to Encounters with The Hugging Molly

The Enchanted Codex: Secrets of the Craft for Witches, Wiccans, and Pagans

Harvest of Gratitude: A Complete Thanksgiving Guide

Yuletide Essentials: A Complete Guide to an Authentic and Magical Christmas

Celestial Smokes: A Cosmic Guide to Cigars and Astrology

Living in Balance: A Comprehensive Survival Guide to Thriving with Diabetes Insipidus

Cosmic Symbiosis: The Venom Zodiac Chronicles

The Cursed Paw of Ambition

Cosmic Symbiosis: The Astrological Venom Journal

Celestial Wonders Unfold: A Stargazer's Guide to the Cosmos (2024-2029)

The Ultimate Black Friday Prepper's Guide: Mastering Shopping Strategies and Savings

Cosmic Sales: The Astrological Guide to Black Friday Shopping

Legends of the Corn Mother and Other Harvest Myths

Whispers of the Harvest: The Corn Mother's Journal

The Evergreen Spellbook

The Doctor Meets the Boogeyman

The White Witch of Rose Hall's SpellBook

The Gingerbread Golem's Shadow: A Study in Sweet Darkness

The Gingerbread Golem Codex: An Academic Exploration of Sweet Myths

The Gingerbread Golem Grimoire: Sweet Magicks and Spells for the Festive Witch

The Curse of the Gingerbread Golem

10-minute Christmas Crafts for kids

Christmas Crisis Solutions: The Ultimate Last-Minute Survival Guide

Gingerbread Golem Recipes: Holiday Treats with a Magical Twist

The Infinite Key: Unlocking Mystical Secrets of the Ages

Enchanted Yule: A Wiccan and Pagan Guide to a Magical and Memorable Season

Dinosaurs of Power: Unlocking Ancient Magick

Astro-Dinos: The Cosmic Guide to Prehistoric Wisdom

Gallifrey's Yule Logs: A Festive Doctor Who Cookbook

The Dino Grimoire: Secrets of Prehistoric Magick

The Gift They Never Knew They Needed

The Gingerbread Golem's Culinary Alchemy: Enchanting Recipes for a Sweetly Dark Feast

A Time Lord Christmas: Holiday Adventures with the Doctor

Krampusproofing Your Home: Defensive Strategies for Yule

Silent Frights: A Collection of Christmas Creepypastas to Chill Your Bones

Santa Raptor's Jolly Carnage: A Dino-Claus Christmas Tale

Prehistoric Palettes: A Dino Wicca Coloring Journey

The Christmas Wishkeeper Chronicles

The Starlight Sleigh: A Holiday Journey

Elf Secrets: The True Magic of the North Pole

Candy Cane Conjurations

Cooking with Kids: Recipes Under 20 Minutes

Doctor Who: The TARDIS Confiscation

The Anxiety First Aid Kit: Quick Tools to Calm Your Mind

Frosty Whispers: A Winter's Tale

The Infinite Key: Unlocking the Secrets to Prosperity, Resilience, and Purpose

The Grasping Void: Why You'll Regret This Purchase

Astrology for Busy Bees: Star Signs Simplified

The Instant Focus Formula: Cut Through the Noise

The Secret Language of Colors: Unlocking the Emotional Codes

Sacred Fossil Chronicles: Blank Journal

The Christmas Cottage Miracle

Feeding Frenzy: Graboid-Inspired Recipes

Manifest in Minutes: The Quick Law of Attraction Guide

The Symbiote Chronicles: Doctor Who's Venomous Journey

Think Tiny, Grow Big: The Minimalist Mindset

The Energy Key: Unlocking Limitless Motivation

New Year, New Magic: Manifesting Your Best Year Yet

Unstoppable You: Mastering Confidence in Minutes

Infinite Energy: The Secret to Never Feeling Drained

Lightning Focus: Mastering the Art of Productivity in a Distracted World

Saturnalia Manifestation Magick: A Guide to Unlocking Abundance During the Solstice

Graboids and Garland: The Ultimate Tremors-Themed Christmas Guide

12 Nights of Holiday Magic

The Power of Pause: 60-Second Mindfulness Practices

The Quick Reset: How to Reclaim Your Life After Burnout

The Shadow Eater: A Tale of Despair and Survival

The Micro-Mastery Method: Transform Your Skills in Just Minutes a Day

Reclaiming Time: How to Live More by Doing Less
Chronovore: The Eternal Nexus
The Mind Reset: Unlocking Your Inner Peace in a Chaotic World
Confidence Code: Building Unshakable Self-Belief
Baby the Vampire Terrier
Baby the Vampire Terrier's Christmas Adventure
Celestial Streams: The Content Creator's Astrology Manual
The Wealth Whisperer: Unlocking Abundance with Everyday Actions
The Energy Equation: Maximize Your Output Without Burning Out
The Happiness Algorithm: Science-Backed Steps to Joyful Living
Stress-Free Success: Achieving Goals Without Anxiety
Mindful Wealth: The New Blueprint for Financial Freedom
The Festive Flavors of New Year: A Culinary Celebration
The Master's Gambit: Keys of Eternal Power
Shadowed Secrets: Groundhog Day Mysteries
Beneath the Burrow: Lessons from the Groundhog
Spring's Whispers: The Groundhog's Prediction
The Limitless Mindset: Unlock Your Untapped Potential
The Focus Funnel: How to Cut Through Chaos and Get Results
Bold Moves: Building Courage to Live on Your Terms
The Daily Shift: Simple Practices for Lasting Transformation
The Quarter-Life Reset: Thriving in Your 20s and 30s
The Art of Shadowplay: Building Your Own Personal Myth
The Eternal Loop: Finding Purpose in Repetition
Burrowing Wisdom: Life Lessons from the Groundhog
Shadow Work: A Groundhog Day Perspective
Love in Bloom: 5-Minute Romantic Gestures
The Shadowspell Codex: Secrets of Forbidden Magick
The Burnout Cure: Finding Balance in a Busy World
The Groundhog Prophecy: Unlocking Seasonal Secrets
Nog Tales: The Spirited History of Eggnog

Six More Weeks: Embracing Seasonal Transitions
The Lumivian Chronicles: Fragments of the Fifth Dimension
Money on Your Mind: A Beginner's Guide to Wealth
The Focus Fix: Breaking Through Distraction
January's Spirit Keepers: Mystical Protectors of the Cold
Creativity Unchained: Unlocking Your Wildest Ideas in 2025
Manifestation Mastery: 365 Days to Rewrite Your Reality
The Groundhog's Mirror: Reflecting on Change
The Weeping Angels' Christmas Curse
Burrowed in Time: A Groundhog Day Journey
Heartbeats: Poems to Share with Your Valentine
Dino Wicca: The Sacred Grimoire of Prehistoric Magick
Courage of the Pride: Finding Your Inner Roar
The Lion's Leap: Bold Moves for Big Results
Healthy Hustle: Achieving Without Overworking
Practical Manifesting: Turning Dreams into Reality in 2025
Jurassic Pharaohs: Unlocking the Magick of Ancient Egypt and Dino Wicca
The Happiness Equation: Small Changes for Big Joy
The Confidence Compass: Finding Your Inner Strength
Whispers in the Hollow: Tales of the Forgotten Beasts
Echoes from the Hollow: The Return of Forgotten Beasts
The Hollow Ascendant: The Rise of the Forgotten Beasts
The Relationship Reset: Building Better Connections
Mastering the Morning: How to Win the Day Before 8 AM
The Shadow's Dance: Groundhog Day Symbolism
Cupid's Kitchen: Quick Valentine's Day Recipes
Valentine's Day on a Budget: Love Without Breaking the Bank
Astrocraft: Aligning the Stars in the World of Minecraft
Forecasting Life: Groundhog Day Reflections
Bleeding Hearts: Twisted Tales of Valentine's Terror
Herbal Smoke Revolution: The Ultimate Guide to Nature's Cigarette Alternative

Winter's Wrath: The Complete Survival Blueprint for Extreme Freezes.

The Groundhog's Shadow: A Tale of Seasons

Burrowed Insights: Wisdom from the Groundhog

Sensual Strings: The Art of Erotic Bondage

Whispered Flames: Unlocking the Power of Fire Play

Forgotten Shadows: A Guide to Cryptids Lost to Time

Six Weeks of Secrets: Groundhog Day's Hidden Messages

Shadows and Cycles: Groundhog Day Reflections

The Art of Love Letters: Crafting the Perfect Message

Romantic Getaways at Home: Turning Your Space into Paradise

Purrfect Brews: A Cat Lover's Guide to Coffee and Companionship

The Groundhog's Wisdom: Timeless Lessons for Modern Life

The Shadow Oracle: Groundhog Day as a Predictor

Emerging from the Burrow: A Journey of Renewal

The Language of Love: Learning Your Partner's Love Style

Authorpreneur: The Ultimate Blueprint for Writing, Publishing, and Thriving as an Author

Weathering the Seasons: Groundhog Day Perspectives

Valentine's Day Magic: A Guide to Romantic Rituals

The Shadow Chronicles: Stories of Groundhog Day

Love and Laughter: Fun Games for Valentine's Day

AstroRealty: Unlocking the Stars for Property Success

The Groundhog's Path: A Guide to Seasonal Balance

Groundhog Day Diaries: Reflections in the Shadow

The Groundhog's Light: Illuminating the Path Ahead

Valentine's Traditions from Around the World

AI Wealth Revolution: Unlocking the Trillionaire Mindset

Love Rekindled: Reigniting Passion in Relationships

Single and Thriving: Self-Love on Valentine's Day

Emerald Legends: Mystical Tales of Ireland

Green Alchemy: Harnessing Nature's Magic

The Hearts of Horror: A Valentine's Day Nightmare

The Leprechaun's Guide to Wealth and Wisdom

Dancing with the Sidhe: Celebrating the Otherworld

Shamrocks and Shadows: Mysteries of the Green Isle

Emerald Energy: Harnessing Luck and Growth

The Gingerbread Golem's Valentine: A Sweetheart's Guide to Love and Enchantment

The Celtic Knot: Weaving Life and Destiny

Green Fire: Elemental Magic for St. Patrick's Day

Clover Chronicles: Finding Your Inner Luck

Ireland's Mystical Creatures: A Field Guide

Gingerbread Golem's Love Almanac

Prowl and Thrive: The Lion's Guide to Success

Love Alchemy: Transforming Your Life Through Heart Energy

WORLD DOMINATION: Woman's Rule 3:The New Life

The Midnight Rose: A Guide to Lunar Love Spells

The Forbidden Letters: Writing Your Own Love Prophecy

Luck and Lore: St. Patrick's Day for Modern Mystics

The Green Path: A Pagan Celebration of Renewal

The Dark Architect's Guide to Reprogramming Reality

Prankster's Paradise: A Guide to Harmless Hijinks

Manifest Your Reality: The Law of Attraction Simplified

The TARDIS Owner's Manual: Understanding the Doctor's Ship: *A complete guide to the TARDIS, its technology, secrets, and mysteries*

Starlit Romance: Astrology Secrets for Finding True Love

The Time Lord's Atlas: A Complete Guide to the Whoniverse: ***A breakdown of the locations, planets, and dimensions explored in Doctor Who***

Sweetheart Shadows: The Dark Side of Love and Attraction

February Fire: Reigniting Passion in Every Area of Life

The Self-Love Toolkit: 5 Ways to Embrace Who You Are
February Sparks: Ignite Your Dreams in 28 Days
March to Success: A 31-Day Action Blueprint
Ancient Paths: The 13 Sacred Principles of Dino Wicca
Echoes of Tomorrow: Navigating the AI Revolution
The Wellness Blueprint: Balancing Mind, Body, and Soul
Green Horizons: Sustainable Living for a Better Tomorrow
The AI Wealth Code: How to Make Millions with Automation
AI-Powered Creativity: Writing, Art, and Music for Profit
Extinction Rites: Rebirthing Your Soul Through Prehistoric Magick
Sacred Serpents tarot
Celestial Enchantment blank journal
Star Strains
Culinary Journeys: Exploring Global Flavors at Home
The Hollowvale Curse
The Hollowvale Harvest
The Egg of Transformation: Awakening Your Inner Power
Blooming Into Power: A Wiccan Guide to Spring Awakening
The Nightmare Nexus: The Third Doctor's Perilous Haunting
Digital Detox: Reclaiming Your Life in a Connected World
Ostara's Path: Walking the Spiral of Renewal
The Sacred Hare
Financial Freedom: Building Wealth in the Modern Age
Spring's Cauldron: Stirring the Waters of Change
The Hollowvale Pact
Quantum Consciousness: The Science of Reality Shifting
The Hollowvale Hunger
The Sacred Waters Within: A Witch's Guide to Hydrocephalus Magick
The Raven's Nest: Building a Life of Unshakable Stability
AI and the Human Mind: The Future of Intelligence
The Hollowvale Reckoning

Timeless Love: Building and Maintaining Lasting Relationships

The Raven's Roar: Unlocking Unstoppable Confidence

Raven Sight: Awakening Intuition and Inner Wisdom

The Butterfly Effect: Small Changes, Big Transformations

Taming the Boogeyman: How to Conquer Your Inner Fears

The Magick of Green: Awakening Earth's Energy in You

The Entrepreneurial Mindset: Secrets to Business Success

The Hollowvale End

The Shadow Luck Ritual: Reclaiming Power from Your Dark Side

Spring Magick for Beginners: A Simple Guide to Seasonal Energy Work

Doctor Who: The Hollowvale Conundrum

The March of Miracles: Unlocking Synchronicities in Spring

Unveiling the Cosmos: A Guide to Stargazing and Space Exploration

The Ultimate Guide to Surviving an Economic Collapse

The AI Gold Rush: How to Profit from the AI Revolution

Bastet's Shadow: The Hidden Power of Feline Magick

The Bastet Codex: Unlocking the Goddess's Magickal Secrets

Purring Spells: Harnessing Bastet's Healing Frequencies

Bastet's Nine Lives: Rebirth, Transformation, and Immortality Spells

Primal Currents: Hydrocephalus Magick in the Path of Dino Wicca

The Digital Gold Rush: Mastering E-Commerce and Online Sales

Future Shock: Adapting to the Next Decade of Change

The Quantum Mindset: Think Like a Billionaire

Sacred Motherhood: Awakening the Divine Feminine Within

The Mother's Spellbook: Enchantments for Love, Protection, and Prosperity

The Witch's Guide to Parenting: Raising Empowered and Intuitive Children

The Magick of Motherhood: Reclaiming Your Power Through Rituals

The Pagan Path to Self-Love: A Goddess's Guide to Worth and Confidence

Wild Woman Magick: Unleashing Your Primal Power

The Money Magnet Blueprint: Unlocking Unlimited Wealth

Biohacking 101: Unlock Your Body's Full Potential

The Wild Father: A Pagan Guide to Strength and Wisdom

The Sacred Masculine: Unlocking Your Inner Power

The Druid's Compass

The Warrior's Mindset

The Father's Fire

Odin's Path

Ancestral Bonds

The House That Whispers

The Magician's Code

The Wild Hunt

The Green Man's Path

The Altar of Success

The Shadow and the Sword

The High Priestess's Guide to Energy Healing

The Lunar Mother

The Sacred Self-Care Grimoire

The Womb Wisdom Codex

The Wheel of the Mother

The Witch's Guide to Manifestation

The Q2 Reset

The Ultimate Guide to AI-Powered Passive Income

Escape the 9-5

AI Feline Fortunes

The Tear-Stained Grimoire

Razorblade Runes
Cemetery Sirens
The Midnight Wristwatch
The Town That Forgets

If you want solar for your home go here: https://www.harborsolar.live/apophisenterprises/

Get Some Tarot cards: https://www.makeplayingcards.com/sell/apophis-occult-shop

Get some shirts: https://www.bonfire.com/store/apophis-shirt-emporium/

<u>Instagrams:</u>
@apophis_enterprises,
@apophisbookemporium,
@apophisscardshop
Twitter: @apophisenterpr1
Tiktok:@apophisenterprise
Youtube: @sg1fan23477, @FiresideRetreatKingdom
Hive: @sg1fan23477
CheeLee: @SG1fan23477

Podcast: Apophis Chat Zone: https://open.spotify.com/show/5zXbrCLEV2xzCp8ybrfHsk?si=fb4d4fdbdce44dec

Newsletter: https://apophiss-newsletter-27c897.beehiiv.com/

If you want to support me or see posts of other projects that I have come over to: **buymeacoffee.com/mpetchinskg**

I post there daily several times a day

Get your Dinowicca or Christmas themed digital products, especially Santa Raptor songs and other musics. Here: **https://sg1fan23477.gumroad.com**

Apophis Yuletide Digital has not only digital Christmas items, but it will have all things with Dinowicca as well as other Digital products.